How to Pass a Degree with Confidence

Anthony Fox

chipmunkapublishing

the mental health publisher

All rights reserved, no part of this publication may be reproduced by any means, electronic, mechanical photocopying, documentary, film or in any other format without prior written permission of the publisher.

Published by

Chipmunkapublishing

PO Box 6872

Brentwood

Essex CM13 1ZT

United Kingdom

http://www.chipmunkapublishing.com

Copyright © Anthony Fox 2011

Chipmunkapublishing gratefully acknowledge the support of Arts Council England.

How to Pass a Degree with Confidence

I want to say thank you to my daughter Colleen and my son Jamie for the encouragement they have given me over the time it has taken me to write this book. I would also like express my thanks to Saffron Newmarch-grant for helping me edit this book.

Anthony Fox

Who am I

"We are all teachers!

Don't let anybody tell you differently.

Here am I thinking to myself: who am I?

Trying to express myself writing words to paper, without crying out,

Trying to express myself with light and clarity,

Without judgement or lies, who am I?

Learn to live with pain or gain.

When asked who am I, in time or judgement day?

We are all teachers.

Don't let anybody tell you differently.

Thoughts with deeds that count exist and say, who am I?

Not more or less, but what I did.

And how it changed the world I met.

When I am gone the love I left behind was who I am!

©Anthony Fox 1999

Anthony Fox

Introduction

I wrote this book as a study guide because I feel that anyone attempting a degree will find it a useful tool towards passing. I felt my experience would help many students achieve what they wanted. In every chapter I have used personal experiences that I think will help reinforce the main points of each topic.

Anthony Fox

It's Never Too Late

I was 42 years old when I made the first steps towards obtaining my degree and just five years later I had graduated. I was a late starter, you could say; I didn't have the opportunity to go to university when I was younger, so being a mature student meant I had the experience and insight to help others. I have compiled this book of my experience and skills I gained through my years at university so that you can reach your goals too. The practicable knowledge of understanding the needs of students I gained as a student representative, a role that gave me first-hand experience of the problems that students face.

As mature or teenage students you will face the same problems overcoming the stress that succeeding will place on you as I had. Maybe this will be the first time that you have faced this kind of stress. Either way, understanding and dealing with stress is about planning for that future success which I will show you through my experience. Every great achievement is about making a plan, a road map for success. I know students lead busy lives, so I have tried to keep this book as minimal as possible. By reading this book you will discover how to gain the success you seek rather than falling prey to failure.

The seed of your potential is unlimited. There exists in all of us much potential to discover. The potential to fulfil your aims and goals is just the beginning of the road of many steps we take along life's journey of discovery. When we unleash our potential and believe in it we will then travel along very different roads to our eventual goals. Embarking on this route to new knowledge will let emerge an inner peace, which allows us to develop a deeper confidence in ourselves.

Success is about understanding failure and also about not worrying if you do. Many successful people will tell you that they have failed lots of times, before they reached what some of their peers would class as success. The conquest of reaching the summit of Mount Everest is an example of how people who failed in their attempts never gave up hope.

Every chapter in this book is written to give you the tools to accomplish your goal of obtaining a higher education qualification. Each chapter is essential reading to master the skills to not only get your degree, but also to excel. One of the main topics I feel is so important is confidence. Many people in general lack confidence in their ability to cope with new challenges that present themselves. I hope through my experience you will learn how to master the skill of inner confidence which will not only help in your studies, but also when dealing with everyday stress. The pressure our friends and family exert on us to succeed can be, for many, an unbearable burden and one that sometimes leads to unnecessary tragedy.

When you have read this book and absorbed the skills and experience you will be better equipped to deal with the trials and tribulations of undertaking a university degree. If you are thinking about taking the challenge of going to university, but haven't yet made up your mind, then maybe after reading this book you will be able to make your decision. Either way, it is never too late to start, just remember I started late in life. Whatever you decide I wish you well and good luck!

Been There Got the T-Shirt

Having survived four different universities and gained my degrees I feel well qualified to wear the t-shirt. The experience of going to university should place you on the road to success. The effort of struggling with course commitments and balancing a hectic social life should provide you with enough confidence to tackle life after university.

Most university graduates find that the experience of achieving their goals gives them the confidence to tackle the world. Some graduates will go on to further their education and others into rewarding careers.

How I Got My T-Shirt

It wouldn't be right to write this book without telling you how I got the t-shirt. So if you have the time I will now tell you the story. I will keep it short because I know students' time is precious, except of course when we're in the student union bar, then we have all the time in the world.

In some ways, it was a lonely road I travelled. There was no one encouraging me along. I had to do it all by myself. I started right at the bottom of the ladder. Every rung was a step closer to my goal. My early years were spent learning how to use databases, spread sheets and desktop publishing and within a year I was taking a diploma in information technology.

In the beginning, I never imagined that I would end up with a Master's in Software Engineering in Artificial Intelligence or indeed an Honours degree in computing.

In fact it all started with that little mouse. My very first introduction to the world of Microsoft was an evening course at a local college, in how to use the Microsoft Windows 95 operating system. Strange really, it's a bit like the acorn to the oak tree. It was 1997 and the mouse was as alien to me as the jolly green giant. Sure, I knew about computers, I'd had a Spectrum Z80 and an Amstrad when they first came out, you communicated with the computer through the keyboard and that was that. I had played with other computers systems as well, but it was just the same QWERTY keyboard.

After a couple of years, I found myself doing a HND in computing, one rung below a degree, which was intensive to say the least. I was learning how to program computers, not just how to build and play with them.

I was surrounded by geeks of all shapes and sizes. Bespectacled I was not, but many were. I was never typical, usually the opposite of everything you assume. You have the loud and the quiet ones and I guess I would be somewhere in the excluded middle. Then there are the ones that just cannot stop talking. Everyone has met them; they're the guys and girls who have more mouth than just about anyone else.

Anyway, I would be listening rather than talking because at times I wasn't sure about Jack shit, but that was me. Sure enough, I passed with flying colours and received a letter from the university principal telling me that I came fourth out of all the HND students that year, which was quite an achievement.

The following year I transferred onto the degree program at Plymouth University and found myself doing a BSc Honours in Computing. It was round two, another rung up the educational ladder. One thing for sure, university life is different and each one was different from the previous. I had already attended a couple of different universities years before, as part of a correspondence course where you study for a degree at home, and then also spend several weeks of the year at a university of your choice. I only did the correspondence course for a couple of years because I found juggling work and home-studying too difficult to manage. I was a family man then, not superman.

It was a shock to go to lectures and tutorials and in some never see a hand go up to ask a question. I guess I had a misplaced TV idea of universities, the place where you went to ask questions and were given answers. Most of the time when I stuck my hand up I was alone among the cream of the crop. It never occurred to me you should just sit there and take some notes, leave, and that was that. That year went fast and I passed with an upper second in my Honours degree, not quite a first but I was still pleased. It had been a struggle at times, but I guess without that it wouldn't have been a challenge.

The summer breaks were welcome and for a short while I chased employment. I could not afford to continue up the educational ladder since I was broke and in debt. That was until the day I saw an advert in a careers brochure advertising free Master courses, available with a bursary at a university the other end of the country. This was my passport to move another step up the educational ladder.

After a gruelling eleven hour drive to Sunderland University, arriving at the post graduate campus with all that I now had left squashed into my car, I had little time to regret the decision I had made. Consoling myself with the reminder that I was not homeless, and at least I had a home for the next year and a half, I soon got into the swing of things and made new friends even though they were mostly half my age or less. I soon joined the university salsa group and some other clubs outside of the university, where at one of these I found myself a girlfriend. I needed some outside distractions away from the stress of studying and the student union bar. It was fun on campus, going on crazy nights out with friends, sometimes lasting until the sun came up the next morning. It was round three, a different level, more like the knock out stage.

This was a different university I was at now, a few more hands went up including mine, but still not as many as I had expected. They were maybe smarter or more embarrassed than me, either way that's the way it was. I ditched my illusion that universities were the places you asked questions; from my experience students didn't ask enough.

Early on, the software engineers voted for me to represent them as their student representative, a role I neither wanted nor coveted at the time. The extra work and time involved is probably the reason why everyone voted for me, and that's how I looked at the role. It turned out to be a blessing in disguise, but I didn't know it at the time. Apparently, students from previous years received poor marks or failed because of not understanding critical analysis. Tutors criticised the lack of understanding of critical analysis by students. These criticisms came up time and again in discussions at academic board meetings that I attended as part of my new role. Tutors explained that it wasn't their role to teach critical analysis and that it was up to the students to learn about it for themselves. Afterwards, I immediately sent an email to all the students I represented, informing them of what I had found out. Thereupon, there was a mad rush that afternoon to the university library to find books on critical thinking and analysis. Luckily, I had a head start.

Don't worry, I explain what critical analysis is later in the book. Besides, I believe many books fail to warn students that there's a bit more meat on the bone when it comes to critical thinking and analysis. Anyway, let me get back to my story. I learnt a lot about student problems as a student rep and I am glad to say I helped many. One thing I did learn is not to be afraid to ask questions; I certainly did.

As the weeks passed, it wasn't long before we were revising for exams while also working on assignments. Creating a study plan became a life saver; I would have been in a complete mess without it those last two months before exams. Talk about manic. I felt like throwing my computer out of the window more times than I have fingers. My box would freeze more often than I can remember. I had less patience with my computer than a dog on heat.

You can call it Sod's Law, Murphy's Law or the Mother-in-law, what could go wrong, did. I was so worried I phoned my tutor and explained I could not test my code for the assignment. He told me not to worry and to just submit my work, which is what I did. It was a dark moment when I felt I would fail, and the stress was manic. I had been locked away for several days in my room, struggling and juggling with computer problems, exam preparation, assignments and time was running out.

So far I had a record of all A's and B's and was working towards a first in my Master's degree in Software Engineering in Artificial Intelligence and I didn't want to fail at the final hurdle. It had been hard work; no easy ride these last few months, the stress was crazy, I knew I couldn't afford to fail.

I was literally broke, just living off a university bursary. There was no second chance for me; I could not afford to retake anything, not a semester, not even a single assignment or module, absolutely sod all. On top of all that I had a girlfriend who was more manic than me at times. It was bad enough that I had a computer reminiscent of a complaining wife that never stops nagging to update. So there I was withdrawing into my interior world, trying to cope without the blessing of a fairy godmother coming to my rescue.

Also, just to ice the cake, I had students coming to me complaining that they couldn't access a particular university server, which was required as part of an assignment due in a couple of days' time. Yes, the server was down more times than it was up. I spoke to the tutor about the server problem requesting some leeway on the due date. He wasn't at all happy about extending the due date for the assignment by three days, but I believe it saved the bacon of many fellow students and also mine. What with some exams and assignments being due on the same date, the extra three days for that assignment gave me and many other students the time to test our work with confidence.

Now with all assignments and exams out of the way it was time to work on the all-important dissertation. Getting a first in your dissertation almost guarantees you a first class masters, providing you have the prerequisite marks in your modules, which I had been working towards throughout the semesters. I had friends who were doing MBA's and other subjects and just because I was older they would come to me for advice. Not that I had the time to scrutinise every line of their objectives. What advice I did give would be the same on any project; make sure that you don't wander off into the bush and that you always understand the task ahead.

I remember one of my friends was a Greek girl called Kiki who was studying for a MBA. One day while on the bus to university I got talking to her about her course, and she explained how it was going. I asked her to tell me in a *word* or *sentence* what was the most important aspect in business. She thought for a moment, and then went on to rattle off several sentences about this and that. It wasn't meant to be a trick question. I just wanted to see what Kiki would say. To be fair, I don't think she thought about it for long enough, but don't forget that I'd spent more time thinking about the question than she did. Besides, my question asked for one word or sentence, not a series of sentences. We can all fall into the trap of not listening and not thinking about what exactly the question asked. I told her the most important aspect in business, in my opinion, is *people*; because it doesn't matter how good the product or service you are selling is, *it's the people that make the difference*. If you have people that are unhappy and can't communicate, well, then your business is ultimately doomed.

So you should do your best to try and fully understand the project objectives and stick to them. It's easy to wander into oblivion, and even harder to stick to the original task. My dissertation took me several months of work to complete, which I enjoyed once I fully understood the task I had set myself.

The day I handed my dissertation in for marking I was relieved that I'd done the best I could in the time allowed and so patted myself on the back. I didn't reach the goal I'd set myself of getting a first. Overall, I was two per cent away from a first, but I was not disappointed, I had passed with flying colours and in doing so had tested myself to the limit.

The journey had been long, with many ups and downs but I still kept going up the ladder even when Sod's Law, Murphy's Law or whatever law you want to call it had crept into the equation. In the end, I had come a long way, since that little mouse had got accustomed to my fingers. So there it is, that's how I got my t-shirt and passed two degrees with confidence.

A Student Perspective

It doesn't matter what age you decide to journey on the road to a university education. I decided to take my degrees in my mature years since I never had the opportunity earlier in my teens. What really matters is the goal and enthusiasm that you need to fully enjoy the experience. I certainly had a great time; even though most of my fellow students were younger than me, this didn't stop me from making friends and enjoying the campus night life.

It wasn't hard to find the student bar and enjoy the cheap beer. In fact, I made the effort of joining student social clubs, which are a great place to meet new people away from your usual colleagues that you find yourself mixing with while on your course.

Having a passion for dancing I joined the student salsa club which was great in two aspects. Firstly, I got to meet new people and secondly I learnt a lot about other places to go dancing, which broadened my knowledge of the city and the surrounding area. I found myself living a varied and busy social life, which helped to lessen the stress and pressure of academic work. There were plenty of late night student parties and all the usual drunken antics, enjoying the excitement of meeting new friends, sometimes going out nearly every week night.

Something that I'd also recommend is becoming involved in representing other students. My fellow students voted for me to represent them as a student rep for the software engineers, which gave me an insight into the many issues that students encounter, and because I attended academic board meetings I gained a good insight into the problems and issues from the university's point of view. I have included a chapter on 'critical thinking' as this became a major problem contributing to students achieving poor results or even failing across all course subjects. I brought this point up several times at academic board meetings – and was told that students should already have the knowledge and skills to master this important prerequisite to passing exams or assignments. The truth is, critical thinking is not taught – alarming I think, considering how important it is to your success of gaining your degree. My advice is that you make sure you fully understand the chapter on 'critical thinking' and practice this skill, which will greatly improve your chance of success at passing exams and assignments.

Another issue that all universities take great pains to impress on you is how they deal with plagiarism, or put simply, the act of copying other people's work. You will hear speech after speech about how they view plagiarism and how harshly they deal with it. Since the Internet is a readily available source of information, many students fall into the trap of simply cutting and pasting other people's work and try passing it off as their own –which is clearly theft. Of course as a student you are expected to do copious amounts of research from all different types of sources- academic journals, papers, books as well as the Internet. But you have to learn that if you use someone else's work you have to correctly acknowledge this by the university academic standards.

I took my master's degree in software engineering in 2004 at the youthful age of 47 years. So it's never too late to have a go. Whenever you decide to embark on a university education, don't rush into making a decision before you are really well prepared.

How to Study

Taking notes should be brief, and only what you feel should be further researched and investigated. Each lecture or tutorial will be different, because of the diverse teaching practices relevant to each tutor.

It's important to ask questions, especially if you need to clarify something the tutor has said, so don't be afraid to ask. From my experience not enough students ask questions, which tends to lead to a boring lecture. It's easy to lose focus while just sitting there listening to an hour long lecture, without any student participation.

An important factor for effective note taking is that you assimilate what you have written down. There's no point in taking notes and then trying to interpret them weeks or even months later. You will need to adopt a pro-active strategy of spending time reviewing and possibly re-writing your notes whereby this will help you assimilate the information more easily and actually learn. Taking this step in copying your notes will help you to re-learn and study better, and encourage your brain to memorize those important notes for later use.

I would not recommend using a laptop to take notes. I much prefer pencil and paper as you can work faster and expand notes into meaningful diagrams and symbols much easier than on a laptop etc. Besides, taking notes on a laptop is inconsistent with my recommendation of re-writing your lecture notes, and also it's a cumbersome accessory to lug around the campus.

In some of your lectures you will find that notes are provided for you either as hand-outs, or available via the web, or in another format such as a PPP file

(Microsoft PowerPoint). It's important not to just read these without making notes; otherwise you will fail to assimilate enough to benefit from these free hand-outs. I found that making your own notes on these hand-outs helped me to learn the key points and was especially useful when it came to exam preparation. Later, I often spent time studying these notes and thinking about key concepts – this helped to understand important concepts and assimilate them into memory.

Most students will have their individual way of studying. This might mean studying in complete silence. Sometimes I prefer to listen to music, and other times to have silence. It's really up to you, deciding what suits you best and which is more conducive to your study time. Again, some students find that there are certain times of the day or night that they can relax and so learn better. Choose a time that suits you best, don't just read your notes passively - by that I mean take the time to stop and think about what you're reading. You should find that this process of thinking about key concepts and ideas will dramatically improve how much you can absorb and learn during one lesson.

If you don't understand a particular sentence or concept either slowly re-read it again or ask a fellow student for an explanation. Failing that you should take note of what you don't understand and make a point of asking your tutor or teacher at the next appropriate time. You must not be afraid to ask questions – you will find many other students will probably be thinking the same. I found asking for explanations outside of lectures and tutorials a very useful task, as this often saved valuable time that would otherwise be wasted trying to figure out the answer. Spending time reading slowly will also help to reinforce your learning and should improve how you memorize information.

There are many methods of highlighting important notes and text – some more useful than others. I find the best way to highlight is to just underline any key words and terms. This method avoids the use of highlighter pens, where you seem to end up highlighting nearly everything and then miss the point of what you are trying to learn. When taking notes I use a type of pseudo code to relate information in a concise yet structured way. The following example demonstrates this technique.

Keyword term (or brief statements)

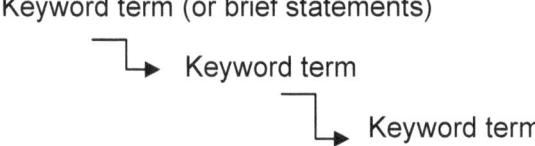

Figure 1: Note Taking Diagram

The idea is to relate key terms together in a logical yet structured manner. If you can make the statements brief, yet expanded enough so that you can follow the information at a later date, such as when you revise for exams, the idea is that you can easily link key concepts and ideas while following the lecture at the same time.

Note: I used this technique for exam revision to assimilate the information more quickly, which allowed more time for other assignments which were often due around the same time.

What to Avoid

The most important thing is that you avoid the spectre of plagiarism while studying for your degree. All universities take special care to inform and instruct their students on how to avoid falling foul of this prevalent academic sickness. Plagiarism is described in the Oxford dictionary as "take and use (another person's ideas, writings or inventions) as one's own". Plagiarism can only be avoided when you fully understand that using other people's intellectual property is theft, and is a common problem in universities. You must remember that not only written words, but also music, art, ideas, computer code and other mathematical and scientific work that you borrow must be fully and accurately cited. This shows that you are quoting the author of the originality and not trying to pass off the work as your own. When you write an essay or construct some computer code, you must pay extra attention to all parts of your work that have been borrowed from other sources, and then attribute each to that author.

There are essentially two forms of plagiarism – one is deliberate, the other accidental. Yet both forms are still wrong and will involve you in unnecessary stress and possible expulsion from your course depending upon the circumstances. Deliberate plagiarism is using others people's work and failing to acknowledge this by not citing the original author. Accidental plagiarism occurs when we fail to accurately attribute another author's work by the standards set by the university. Throughout your course of study you will be informed of the correct standards to use for your attributions of other author's work.

How to Correctly Reference

It is well known that you should always cite the original author and not the author who is reporting the original author. The following example explains this.

Example: Author (X) states that the findings of Author (Y) were the main contributing factors in the document. Yet, you should only cite the original author (Y) in your document. This will require you to seek out the original document of Author (Y), and insert the correct citation and reference of Author (Y) in your document. So remember you need to cite the original author, not the author who is referring to the original author.

The following examples follow the Harvard referencing system standard and should give you an understanding of how best to fully attribute your work.

Example 1: Bryant (2000) questions whether software engineering is really engineering at all, based on its immaturity and undeveloped practices. However, Raccoon et al., (1998) argues that traditional engineering disciplines command legal standing and certification based on well-developed principles and standards of practice.

Example 2: Gotterbarn et al., (1999b) reports that "…the health, safety, and welfare of the public is primary…" and this code is about maintaining public confidence.

Example 3: In order to clarify the debate as to whether software engineering could be classed as an engineering discipline, various engineering text books were consulted, (Pressman 2001; Sommerville 2001;

Peters & Pedrycz, 2000; Petroski 1992; Rolt 1988; Salvadori 1990; Standage 1998) and as a result the author created Table 3 below to represent a sample of the commonalities between software engineering and the traditional engineering fields.

Example 4: Quality improvements derived from using SPI are important; also for limiting the number of defects in the past which have allowed viruses and worms to infect computer systems costing millions in economic damage worldwide. For instance, Peslak (2004) reports, that the 'I Love You' virus was estimated to have cost $6.7 billion in the year 2000 in damages.

Example 5: Recent announcements by leading government officials in order to drive market forces to improve the security of software systems are laudable. Verton (2002) quotes Richard Clarke saying the US government "...will create a market force that will drive security..." It currently spends $20 billion annually on software products.

Example 6: Berstein & Klapphoiz (2001) in their study of software engineering makes an important point, often overlooked, which is that consistent and up to date documentation is essential in the light of practical problems of likely staff changes occurring in any project size.

Example 7: Currently the UK government is committed to 100 major IT projects with an estimated expenditure of £10 billion in 2003/04 (Direct.gov.uk, 2003), therefore a portion of this public money could be allocated for the formation of a software institute.

Example 8: The SWEBOK report advocates the legitimisation of software engineering as a profession and a move towards the licensing of practitioners

(SWEBOK.org, 2004), although there are risks to the licensing issue, as highlighted in section 2.3.3 of this document.

In a reference section somewhere near the back of your project or dissertation you would list the full reference of the attribution. The following references allow anyone to find the appropriate reference should they wish to check your information. You would list your references in alphabetical order, allowing ease of reference for any reader.

References:

Berstein, L. & Klapphoiz, D. (2001) *Teaching old software dogs, old tricks*. ACM SIGSOFT Software Engineering Notes. ACM Press New York, NY, USA .Vol. 26 .Issue 2 (March) pp.33-34

Bryant. A. (2000). *It's engineering Jim ... but not as we know it: software engineering — solution to the software crisis, or part of the problem?* International Conference on Software Engineering. Proceedings of the 22nd international conference on Software engineering. ACM Press New York, NY, USA .pp 78- 87

Direct.gov.uk (2003) Government IT projects. Parliamentary Office of science and technology. July 2003 Number 200 Report Summary. Available online: http://search.direct.gov.uk/ExternalLink?EXTERNAL_LINK=http%3A//www.parliament.uk/post/pn200.pdf Accessed: 31/08/04

Note: It's important to list the date the information was accessed by you for an Internet source.

Gotterbarn, DMiller, K., Rogerson, S. (1999b). *Software engineering code of ethics is approved.* Communications of the ACM. ACM Press New York, NY, USA. Vol. 42, Issue 10 (October).pp 102-107.

Peslak, R. A. (2004). *Improving software quality: an ethics based approach.* Special Interest Group on Computer Personnel Research Annual Conference. Proceedings of the 2004 conference on Computer personnel research: Careers, culture, and ethics in a networked environment. SESSION: Panel on ethics. ACM Press New York, NY, USA.pp.144-150.

Pressman, S. R. (2001). *Software Engineering: A practitioner's approach.* 5thEd. McGraw-Hill. New York, NY, USA.

SWEBOK.org, (2004). Guide to the Software Engineering Body of Knowledge. A project of the Software Engineering Coordinating Committee (a Joint IEEE Computer Society –ACM Committee. Available at:http://www.swebok.org/
Accessed: 06/08/04

Verton, D. (2002). *Cybersecurity Czar Takes Stand on Software Quality.* Computerworld,(August,5).Available:http://www.computerworld.com/securitytopics/security/story/0,10801,73245,00.html Accessed: 26/08/04

There are various styles within a particular standard which you may feel more comfortable with using. Whichever suits you best and what is expected from your tutors should be adopted. After you adopt proper attribution you will find it easy to be confident about conveying your ideas with the concepts and thoughts of other authors.

note: It's important to cite your work correctly using the original author's ideas, concepts or findings, but also equally to have your own critical evaluation. The following example illustrates this point.

Example: Harris (1999) found that 25% of the population of the world suffered with a chronic condition or disease such as cancer. Although Harris' (1999) findings are a useful indication of chronic disease they may not be relied on, because the initial findings do not take into account such variables as culture and environmental differences. For instance, Harris (1999) does not mention the cultural and environmental differences between western and eastern societies. Western societies eat primarily a meat based diet whereas eastern societies eat a primarily vegetarian based diet.

Note: Can you see how your critical evaluation and thoughts could be used? You could go on with your critique by offering the reader some evidence of your thoughts with the following.

Example: Brown et al., (1997) have found compelling evidence in their studies to suggest there is a causal link between national diets and the likely disease that would be common to that society.

I found the best way of forming an essay or assignment was by researching the subject and making notes of ideas and quotes of authors and compiling these into a notebook.

By compiling notes of quotes and concepts it was relatively straightforward to incorporate these into my work because I knew where the source came from and what page etc. It's important to keep an accurate record of attribution which greatly helps you reuse and document the source at a later date. You will find this one of the best methods to use, especially when you come to compile a dissertation which will involve a considerable amount of time and effort combined with organizational skills.

Another form of plagiarism is using one's friends as a source of original work. Many students will often be asked by their fellow students for help which is fine, but you must draw the line at sharing the same work. Passing your work off as your own when it has come from a fellow student will only end in tears. The whole point of taking a degree is to test you academically – pass or fail, it will be your work that counts. If you follow the ideas presented in this book you will dramatically increase your chances of passing a degree with confidence.

Remember that using other people's work is fine as long as you fully cite and attribute that contribution to your work. What universities are looking for when they mark your work is your original thoughts and how well you have understood the ideas and concepts of other authors.

Take the following example concerning computer code.

It is well known that 're-inventing the wheel' is a common expression used by computer programmers, which means that certain well known sub routines are re-used all the time and not re-invented each time the problem needs to be solved. By using well tested sub routines we are not re-inventing the wheel each time the problem occurs. But it's still most important that we cite and attribute the source of this code even if we have made slight adjustments to the original – this way we are showing our indebtedness to the source and at the same time allowing others the ability to mark our work for its construction.

The proliferation of the Internet has made information more readily available, yet conversely plagiarism more prevalent at universities. There is software available to academics that can easily detect and track the existence of plagiarised material which has been directly sourced from the World Wide Web. Even without using this software for detecting plagiarised material, academics can easily tell from the style and level of grammar and language used whether the student has plagiarised from other sources such as books and academic papers etc.

Note: It doesn't take much to tell a cat amongst a pack of dogs.

The Golden Rule

Let me tell you a story to show how important it is to keep your work under lock and key, so to speak. One day I was so busy unravelling the machinations of the problems I was having with some programming code, that I almost forgot the golden rule I had set myself some years earlier. Sure, we all like short cuts, but not when it involves plagiarism, or to put it bluntly, cheating. I believe there aren't any short cuts in life. Anyway, I got a call from a friend of mine doing the same master's course in Software Engineering, asking if he could come over and take a look at what I was doing in a particular assignment, as it happened, the same assignment that was causing me so much heartache. Yes, come over, I said. He duly arrived and I showed him what I was doing. Fair enough in my book, after all, what are friends for if not to help where you can? But he wanted me to cross the line of the golden rule I'd set myself several years before, which I wasn't prepared to do, even though it crossed my mind and my friend seemed such a desperate desperado. He wanted me to send him my code. *No way Jose.*

I had been proven gullible a few years earlier while I was studying for a HND (Higher National Diploma) in computing. I had a friend who took my code lock, stock and too bloody late, and submitted it as his own. What happened then was that when the tutor came to mark the assignment there were two identical pieces of programming code except signed by different authors. Before I knew it we'd both failed and consequently had to re-take both the module assignments during the summer break. The university came down very hard on us, and rightly so. Even though I had unwittingly allowed this student to plagiarise my work, my tutor was most understanding of my predicament. But bound by the university rules he still had no choice other than to fail us both for this breach of student conduct. Don't let your friendship cloud your judgement, that's the moral of that story. I'm not saying you shouldn't ever help your fellow students, but just by explaining what you have done or quickly showing them your work, but never actually give them your work to use as research, which could tempt them into copying your work without you knowing about it.

Anyway, back to my friend, to whom I refused to send that code. Once several days had passed I asked him how he was doing in the assignment and with a beaming smile he said, *'I've copied some code from the internet'* and that he planned to then submit this as his actual assignment. I advised him there and then not to do it, but he went ahead anyway, somehow thinking he wouldn't get caught. But that's not the point. Whether you get caught or not you are still cheating, yet you're only cheating yourself. Besides, the tutors can tell a cat amongst a pack of dogs as easily I can say, *'yippee ki kay.'*

There were other occasions while studying for my master's degree that fellow students and friends asked me, even though I'd refuse, to send them my code, but I offered to show them what I had done. This way I was protecting myself, by not allowing the temptation of others to plagiarise, while also helping people who were having the same problem that I had had not long before.

As for my friend who showed his code to me, which was clearly sourced from the Internet, yet who wasn't prepared to fully attribute where the code came from, well I told him that what he was doing was plagiarism. Which, I explained, meant that if he didn't fully attribute and cite any sources when submitting the work, he would most likely fail. But he didn't listen. He got caught for plagiarism because he failed to attribute the code; thereupon, he failed the assignment and was then seen during the summer break re-taking the assignment. Added to this is the record of this episode on his final year results, which is not good when you wish to present this record to a future employer. So there it is, you know what not to do now!

The Need To Set Goals

No one ever achieved anything worthwhile without first visualising their goals and then writing them down. You don't set out to climb Everest without having the goal to accomplish this task. A key ingredient of success is having the ability to have a vision of what it is you want and how exactly you plan to achieve this aim.

Each step of the academic ladder that I have achieved was made by setting goals. Setting something to aim for is a powerful self-motivator that helps to guide and push us towards reaching our goals.

It's important to set realistic goals, yet set them high enough so that in order to complete them you're going to be personally challenged to push yourself. A key point in goal setting is that you use a time limit for your goals. This sets the scene and helps to focus the mind towards achieving and sub-consciously affirms want you want and what you need to do.

When I did my BSc degree I set myself the goal of achieving a first class degree. Although I didn't quite get there I still achieved a very high standard. I also did the same when I did my master's degree, again just missing a first class. But I did achieve a high standard, which I set for myself throughout my time at university. If I had not set these high goals then the more likely result would be not having achieved so much.

Nobody ever achieved success without having first identified their goals. Early on I decided that I wanted to achieve a first class degree. Setting your sights high and working towards that goal helps. you achieve what you want.

How to Identify Your Goals

Think about how immediate your goals are – whether they're long term or short term. By identifying your goals you can easily see how long they might take to achieve. It might be sensible to write these out on paper so you know what you need to do.

Ascertaining whether your goals are short or long term will allow you to set your priorities more effectively. Once you are aware of what it is that you want to achieve, goal setting becomes much more fun and allows you to express what really matters to you. Confidence in goal setting becomes second nature. If you don't identify and set goals it becomes difficult to achieve that degree, because obtaining your degree will involve several integral steps – like doing assignments and passing exams which form part of the course.

Equally, the purpose of writing down your goals will help you to focus on what is important in your life. I personally set goals throughout my time at university, because I realised that it helped me to focus my efforts in a more constructive way. Your confidence builds as you achieve your goals, even the smaller ones. Doing this will help you to achieve your major aim of obtaining a degree with confidence.

Set your Goals Effectively

It's much better to make goals in a positive statement – like I want to achieve a high mark for this assignment or pass that exam with flying colours. Always try to set your goals at realistic levels that challenge your abilities, but not so high that they are unachievable. Be specific as much as possible while setting your goals, with dates and time limits on how long it will take you to achieve your aims. Begin to write down your goals and prioritise them, so that you can focus more of your attention on those with a higher priority or that will mean more to your confidence in achieving them.

Try to set goals that are part of a much larger long term goal. Passing an exam, for example, requires you to spend time studying and preparing - so you should aim for smaller goals, like keeping to set study times to learn key concepts in preparation for your exam. Doing this will boost your confidence as you reach each target along the way of achieving that main goal. Each time you achieve one of your smaller goals you should affirm your achievement by rewarding yourself. This reward could be just saying out loud 'I have achieved this goal', or buy a takeaway meal; anything that rewards your achievement.

Personal Performance

As with all academic work and study you will benefit from analysing and reflecting on your performance as each goal is achieved. Decide where you could have done better and improve your performance for the next goal. By reflecting on your performance you will be able see where you might need to improve. It's important when setting your goals that they are within your control and are determined by your performance. For example, achieving a pass mark on an assignment is within your control as it is based on your performance. Whereas getting a top mark may be outside of your control because the tutor might decide not to give an A grade to any student not within their range of marks available, regardless of how worthy the assignment.

This happened to me, so I personally set my goal in this assignment as being one of the students who will achieve a good mark of around 60%. I not only did I reach my goal but I exceeded it with my mark of 62% which definitely boosted my confidence. The same tutor also made a similar statement in regard to passing his module – *'don't expect a first, you will be doing well if you pass the module,'* he said. As it turned out, I scored 64% in the exam which was a very high score considering his remarks and his particular marking standards. Overall I passed the module with confidence.

For example:

- You might need to improve your time management.

- Improve your writing skills.

- Acquire more information and knowledge.

- Decide upon what other resources you need to achieve these goals.

- Is there a better way of doing things?

- Better preparation.

- Decide if there is anything blocking your progress for next time.

Have confidence in your ability to achieve the goals that you set for yourself. The more you get acquainted with setting performance goals the closer you'll become to getting what you desire. Remember to always do your best and say to yourself my best is good enough. By affirming to yourself your abilities, you will build your confidence in obtaining what you want – remembering that confidence is a learnt experience and anyone can develop their confidence through setting and achieving their goals.

The idea that self-confidence comes from conquering your fears is something that all people can all relate to. It is a wonderful free feeling when you achieve a goal that you've set for yourself.

Score More Goals than Casanova

I remember playing in the university five a side soccer team for our course; I wasn't a Casanova for sure, although plenty were. Let me tell you a story which is set in my final year as an undergraduate, while doing a BSc in computing at Plymouth University. I think it's important because it's all about goals.

One of the modules I chose to take was mobile communications, specifically about understanding radio frequencies and all that jazz.

Well, our tutor was a bit of a maverick, a likeable heavyweight but with the enthusiasm that would knock you sideways as you listened to his predictions about future technology advances. He was hands on, in the sense that he would encourage questions, and he always had time for his students. But he also ran a strict regime within which he was no soft touch. His tutorials and lectures meant business; if you weren't listening he might ask you a question and if you didn't have a reasonable answer you would look a jerk in front of your peers.

To be fair though, he told you right at the beginning that if you didn't keep up, you would quickly fall behind and not be able to pass the module. Sometimes, after he asked a question, it would be a few seconds before two or three people from a class of 50 might put their hand up. The module was mostly about mathematics and decibels and how radio waves work, which was all new to me. I found it interesting though, but it was still a challenge. It was good that he made you think and didn't just give you the answers to problems, something that was to trigger my mind later when I was researching my dissertation which I talk about in another chapter.

He had an infectious enthusiasm for problem solving and specifically for understanding the engineering requirements for radio communication, whether it's a paging device, satellite communications, a mobile phone system or any other systems that involves radio wave frequencies.

We spent days working on *cost budget analysis* which sounds like an accountant's phrase for adding up the bottom line, but it isn't. The cost budget analysis turned out to be a set of complicated mathematics for determining how a radio communication system will perform in the real world.

We could, for example, see why a satellite phone system that costs billions of dollars to implement would ultimately fail, and this was currently on the market. The satellite phone system used a low stationary orbit which meant you needed more satellites to cover the earth, whereas satellites higher in orbit would cover more of the earth due to the curvature of the earth and also due to how radio waves are directional. But there's the rub; the higher you go the more power you need to generate and receive the signal.

Radio frequencies are directly proportionate to distance, which means they lose signal strength over distance and therefore that's why you see people having to go outside to get a signal on their mobile phone or even worse, having to climb a mountain. This satellite phone system worked on line-of-site and wasn't very practicable if you're in the Andes or in a concrete jungle like New York City. The satellite company went bust, eventually losing billions of dollars for its investors.

If only those pension fund people had talked to a communications engineer before investing their money, or should I say someone else's money. After all, it should have been the pension funds goal to look after granny's savings.

When it came to exam preparation our larger than life tutor explained that understanding *cost budget analysis* implications would form a major part of our exam. He was even kind enough to provide some past exam papers with which we could practice. It wasn't just the mathematics that you needed to understand, but also the practicality of the systems under review. So a decimal in the wrong place could mean you were totally on the wrong track, in terms of your analysis and mathematical skills.

My goal was to practice the mathematics and become familiar with any scenario, which meant several days learning every which way. I had the mathematics down to about twenty minutes for any example, which was pretty good when I knew we had three questions to answer in an hour and a half exam. It needed to be, because it was easy to misplace a decimal point here and there and thus be totally wrong, not only with the mathematics but with your practical analysis as well.

It was a tough goal to meet, especially as the tutor had thrown an extra spanner into the works. I can remember him saying right at the beginning of the module; "Don't expect a first since you'll be doing well if you even pass the module." He told us that a high percentage fail the module every year, roughly 25%. I quickly scanned the room and making a rough calculation I figured that out of fifty students around one in five or more would fail. Looking around at my four friends I thought: *One of us is going to fail*. This is why I decided that I needed to set my goals high as I knew it was going to be tough.

As it turned out, I scored 64% in the exam which was a very high score, considering the tutor's particular remarks and his tough marking standards. So you can see it would be unrealistic to set your goal to achieve a first and then be disappointed when you don't reach it, because some things are outside of your control. But that said, I would still always set my goals high.

How to Build Confidence

Confidence is a theme that I feel is important I discuss. Many of us lack confidence at different times in our lives. Some of us will say, "I totally lack confidence." They are like egomaniacs; they blow everything out of proportion as if they're living under a microscope. Confidence can come and go just like that focus of the microscope.

Confidence can also change depending on our mood. Sometimes we feel good, so naturally our confidence is high, yet sometimes it hits rock bottom when we feel down or depressed. So confidence is not a characteristic that is built into our personalities. We all want to be that person we imagine that has confidence in any scenario, being able to socialise, at that job interview, chatting up girls or boys and just being able to handle anything that comes our way. We all wish we could be a more confident person to help improve our everyday lives. Certainly we don't want to be that person in the corner hiding. We want to be at the front of the class, ready and confident to put our hands up, not worried what people may think, just feeling happy about who we are.

Confidence is a skill, and just like any other it can be taught and mastered. If you are wondering at this moment whether you should go on to higher education, with the nagging doubt: Will it be worth it? ask yourself this question, Am I doing it for me? What I am trying to address is that many people do things, not for themselves, but because they feel expected to, from friends or parents. Challenge yourself for you, and not for someone else. Experience has taught me that success is built on three main attributes; personality, enthusiasm and confidence.

Each and every one of us has been given many gifts as well as one special gift, and that is life itself. The challenge we have is to reach for the stars and experience as many gifts that will not only enlighten our lives, but also help change the world to be a better place. This book is about my experience and how I found new confidence. Some people lack the confidence and so they never extend themselves into areas of new knowledge and understanding, because they often fear failure.

You have to learn to be confident before you can succeed in what you want to achieve. There are many times in our lives when we may feel less confident with our ability to cope, but this is usually more to do with the fear of failing rather than the lack of confidence. I will attempt to give you the confidence that you need to be able to achieve your aim of getting that degree, but along the way I also hope you will gain the confidence that will enable you to cope in other aspects of your life.

I have divided the task of improving your confidence into a series of steps which should be fun, and even if you are already a fairly confident person these steps should strengthen your skills.

Confidence Building

Even a confident person will sometimes have doubts about their ability; it's in the human nature and is acceptable.

Step 1: Do Not Fear Failure

Take a simple task that you have never attempted before. For example: You could ask someone you like out for a date - without worrying about whether they say yes or no.

Another example: Attempt a task in which you feel you have no skill, such as drawing or painting a picture. Again don't worry about how it may come out like. I have been painting and drawing for many years and I still find that not everything I paint or draw turns out to be a masterpiece. I believe this to be the same for many artists, even the great masters.

You may have already attempted one of these examples, but my point is to try and challenge yourself to something you have never done before without worrying about the outcome.

Step 2: Self Analysis

From step 1 analyse your progress. Did you find the tasks you chose easy to tackle or difficult? If you found the tasks easy then maybe you should try something else. Write down how you felt doing these tasks. Don't worry if you got the wrong response, for example or if you didn't paint that perfect picture. What's more important is that you gave it a go.

It would be a good idea to repeat and get used to challenging yourself to unfamiliar tasks. Do not worry about failure or what people might think. At each stage analyse and evaluate your progress and give yourself encouragement and praise.

After each step self-evaluate and ask a friend about how they thought you performed. Again, don't worry whether they criticise or praise your efforts. Self-analysis is more important than what your friends might have said. The first step in confidence building is to overcome fear as well as criticism. The most successful people are often individuals who have learnt not to fear these things. The second point here is that criticism is often biased, but you can learn to take the good from the bad and therefore improve your confidence or skill.

Step 3: Join a Group
Now join a group such as an amateur dramatic society, a chess club, sports club, book reading group or any other group that maybe you have thought about in the past. Whichever local club or group you join, take part in as many of the activities that they organise as you can. This process of joining a group is to help build your self-confidence by developing your group skills.

Working in groups is important in helping you learn to cope with dealing with people, and not just yourself. Being challenged by people you are unfamiliar with will help build your confidence and allow you to move in different circles. By joining a group you have no option but to make new friends and acquaintances, which is good practice while building your self-confidence.

Step 4: Embrace Success

Confidence is not something you are born with, it increases as you learn and grow and can also decrease at certain points in your life. As a child your parents instil confidence in you by praising the things you do well, but you can also teach yourself confidence. From this praise and from knowing that we did our best and that our best is good enough we can thus learn self-confidence.

I would say that the art of success or of being a winner is gained through not being afraid to lose. The more we try and gain successful experience, the further our self-confidence is strengthened. Being self-confident is not about an indifference to the world around you or about having a blasé attitude as if nothing matters but yourself. If you stick your head in the sand believing that you are always right and everyone else is wrong, it's more likely that you have difficulty coping and your apparent self-confidence is a mirage of sand built on arrogance.

By attempting new tasks regardless of whether you succeed or fail you are using a strategy destined for future success. Any road to success is always going to be hard, but once you make the first step the journey becomes easier; as Confucius said, "*a journey of a thousand miles begins with a single step.*"

We have to learn to embrace success and praise ourselves more, learning that not everything we do will be a masterpiece or we won't always succeed. Often what you produce is not up to your normal standard, whatever that might be. Some of the best and most creative inventors and artists have found their inspirations by chance.

Conclusion

Self-belief allows us to cope in any situation; it gives us the ability to manage failure, as part of the road to a successful outcome. An athlete may compete in many events yet only win a few, it's part of the course. Therefore the key to achieving self-confidence is recognising that not all the activities we attempt might not turn out to be a success and that we shouldn't dwell on any negative results. Success comes to those that keep trying, and self-confidence maintains our enjoyment until we reach that goal.

The importance of self-analysis is more important than what your friends might have said. The first step in confidence building is to overcome the fear of failure and also the criticism that might come from your efforts. The most successful people are often individuals who have learnt not to fear failure and disapproval. The second point here is criticism; although it's often biased you can also learn to take the good from the bad, and, therefore, improve your confidence or skill.

It's important to learn self-belief whether one succeeds or not in something we attempt. Part of learning self-confidence is the ability to try. It's not about the eventual outcome, more important is our demeanour and not worrying about what people might think and just enjoying ourselves.

So to sum up I would say give it a go, try new things, don't be afraid of what people might think and keep building your confidence even if some days you might feel as though you have none. I believe these are only temporary blimps, you can always think about the other things you have tried and your inner confidence will return. Learn to praise other people as well as yourself; as this will also help to build your self-belief too.

To Be or Not to Be

Now, here is a story of how I didn't let my confidence down. I had just joined the university salsa club, one of my ways of making new friends while also keeping fit for the task ahead. Even though pretty much everyone was half my age, I didn't let it get me down. I already knew how to salsa as one of my previous girlfriends had introduced me to its affectionate ways and we had spent many a time dancing the night away in various clubs, locally as well further out around the country.

I knew I needed to keep fit because I would be spending many hours labouring over the computer keyboard over the next year or so, while I set about the task of achieving a master's in Software Engineering in Artificial Intelligence. Stuck at the other side of England way up north in freezing Sunderland it was as alien to me as finding a rabbi in a Muslim mosque. The locals seemed as mad as hatters, the young teenage girls and boys stripping down to not much except their waistline, and they would walk around from pub to pub as if it were a tropical climate, instead of this chilling freeze from the northern arctic. It was a practice I had never seen before; they say they're hard up north where the women drink pints and the men drink more. I certainly believe that's true.

As the weeks passed by I enjoyed my nights in the groove of the salsa beats. It was a world away from the usual computer code and neural networks. It wasn't long before I was venturing further in the quest to seek the pleasures of the South American samba. Sure enough, one night I met a lass who moved across the dance floor with the rhythm of the samba and re-charged my batteries at the same time. Jill was her name, and I was her Jack, and up and down we would play to the salsa dance floor beats. She was a career woman and in some ways more confident than me; at the time I was just a student struggling to pay my way through university, sometimes with less money in my pocket than a beggar on the street. Did I pick her up or did she pick me up? I'm not so sure, either way I don't think it matters. The first time we went back to her place she drove for half an hour from her place to the campus to pick me up. She was a girl that made so much noise I couldn't keep her mouth shut, I thought the neighbours would hear us it was that loud. But that was Jill, polite, but ready to jump to the front of the queue. The weekends were the only time I really got to see Jill; I was too busy tapping away on my keyboard during the week. Besides, I would spend the odd night in the student union bar with my younger friends around the corner. To say they liked to drink would be an understatement. Many a night I would stagger the few steps back to my campus room, just as the sun came up the next day. But I have no regrets, I did enjoy myself while I worked hard and sometimes played even harder.

It was one of these nights when I really showed my friends and myself the confidence that I really had. The university salsa club had arranged a dance party at the nearby student union bar. Jill and I went along and it was packed with people, all my friends were there, you couldn't move unless you were on the dance floor. The music was blasting to the salsa beat and everybody who was anyone was on the dance floor moving their stuff. Jill and I soon made a bee-line for the floor and we just rocked baby hitting those beats, it was just magic. My friends couldn't believe what they saw, they didn't realise I could dance. So many different girls wanted to dance with me, yet for one thing I didn't have the energy, and for another I was worried about how jealous

Jill would get. One thing is for sure though; I really felt my confidence go up several notches. It was great!

How to Cope With Stress

Stress is an unseen and often neglected problem and is often overlooked by both students and academics. Most people suffer with stress at one point or another, but don't realise they have it. It can affect everyone in different ways, sometimes with anger, depression or causing illness. I have included this chapter on stress because many students do experience this yet may not always know how to deal effectively with the problem.

There's always a balance in life's mission of work and play. Yes, achieving your goals should be important to you, but not if at the expense of your well-being. Setting goals because of what other people might expect of you and not because that is what you want is an example of the wrong reason to push yourself.

You have to enjoy what you are doing and want to do it for yourself. So when stress does build up make time for relieving this by doing things away from your studies. Always remember to keep a happy balance of work and play.

Stress Management

Stress manifests itself when we forget to look after and neglect ourselves. This could take the form of participating in sport activities, meeting friends or simply doing something that you enjoy doing like a hobby. Joining the local salsa club while at university gave me the chance to unwind and make new friends. You will be surprised at how many university clubs are available to you locally.

Note: Managing stress is just half the battle, the other half is learning to ask questions and seek help. Make a study time plan to lessen the stress of coping with assignments and exams. I found planning my study time an important tool in managing my work load; without it I would have been lost. Some weeks I needed the study plan just to make sure I devoted enough time to each subject. This strategy helped me achieve a set of high course grades.

Understanding Stress

Stress is a potential killer. Finding ways to avoid stress will help lighten the load of dealing with other things like exams, assessments, and presentations. One way of relieving stress is by exercising regularly, which also helps in maintaining that healthy balance between study and play.

Note: There were plenty of times when I felt like giving up; however, I never did, I just kept on going. The university campus can sometimes be a stressful environment and making sure I spent enough time away from it was one method that helped me to cope.

Seeking Help with Stress

If you find you just can't cope with all the stress you have in your life then it's advisable to seek help. The university usually has professional counsellors which can help with most problems that can be experienced by students.

Ask to see your student representative. This person is your link to so much information which might be helpful while dealing with any stress in the future.

Whatever you do, make sure you get the help you need and you don't suffer in silence. It always saddens me when I hear about students that have got so weighed down by it all that they've ended up committing suicide. Whatever problem might arise, there will always be a way out. Until then remember there is always tomorrow and that help could be just around the corner.

Do not feel ashamed about asking for help managing your stress as we all suffer with it at some time, in one form or another. We all need to ask someone for help at least once in our lives. So please don't hesitate to seek help if you start finding it all too hard.

Note: I was lucky having a lot of contacts from being a student rep, which meant I knew where to go if I needed some advice or support. Personally, I found that talking to my course tutor about difficulties and issues helped me. It doesn't matter how big or small your problems are; it's always better to share them with someone and get a second opinion when dealing with them.

More Stress than a Chain Smoking Nurse

There was a time during university when I had more stress than a chain smoking nurse in a non-smoking hospital. It doesn't matter when that stress occurs, it's as real as it gets, bread and butter reality. I was struggling with a computer that wouldn't behave while juggling with assignments and revision for exams when the stress that crept up on me made me feel like a zombie and my eyeballs were popping mad. Everyone who has used a computer must have experienced problems which were like those nightmares that wouldn't go away. I could have rolled into a corner until my nightmare was over.

They say when things go wrong it usually happens in threes, well multiply what you like because it felt like my whole world was crashing down upon me in numbers. I wasn't superman, just a man who hadn't so much as a shoulder to cry on. I had given it my best throughout the year so far and done well by all accounts. So pull up a seat you coffee junkies, milkshake hussies and telly-tubbies because this is a story almost certain to make your hair curl. At the time I had fairly straight hair, but I felt as if my hair was curling with every minute that passed. I could have thrown my computer straight out the window more times than I can count the fingers on my hands and bought a hair dryer instead.

Give me an Olympic medal for effort, as there were more things going wrong than there were things going right and I was slap bang in the middle of it all. Stress had slapped me in the face so much that I didn't know whether I would make it to the next round. There were days when I had to work virtually around the clock; I had no choice as time was running out. My computer system had let me down big time and it froze more times than I care to remember, wasting valuable time within my tight study plan.

It was three days before my final course exam and I had an assignment due the same day. I couldn't test the code I had written, my whole time management plan was being torpedoed, and I was sunk as to what to do. I knew my code ran OK, because I'd tested it on university servers, but I couldn't spare enough time to be able to trot off to the university every time I ran some code. On top of this I also needed to find time to revise for final exams in my post graduate digs, my haven.

The stress and the time that I wasted dealing with one assignment over-spilt on whether I had done enough in other assignments due in around the same time. On top of that I had final year exams to revise for in which I couldn't afford the time lapse.

The stress was manic and at times I felt like I would explode but I knew I just couldn't give up. I tried everything, even re-installing software, but I guess I didn't know what the problem was and I didn't have the time to sit back and try to figure it out. One thing I was sure of was that the machine needed more memory, but I didn't have the money or the time to fix it, I just had to live with it and that was that. I knew the real problem was the Java OS which wasn't behaving as it should, as the application I had written was in Java source code and ran fine on the university's test servers. The problem was my machine, which had a habit of turning blue and freezing which was an issue of my computer's OS (Operating System) used at the time.

Besides, now I only had a couple of days left before the assignment was due in and an exam on the same day to sweat over. I had to somehow forget about the issue and try to concentrate on my study plan. It was one of my darkest moments caused by the stress of everything building up when at times I felt like collapsing, luckily though I had made a study and revision plan and without it I would have been in an even worse mess.

On top of that, call it what you like Sod's Law, Murphy's Law or the poor old Mother-in-law, what could go wrong did. I had a girlfriend that was more manic than me. One minute she was phoning to say she wanted to finish with me, and I replied, "*That's OK. I haven't got the time anyway.*" Two hours later she phones back to say she'd been a bit hasty and really she wanted to still continue with the relationship. Life was certainly interesting, if a little stressful.

In the end, I phoned my tutor and explained the scenario about the code that I couldn't test on my box. He told me not to worry and just submit my work, which is what I did. I coped with the stress even when I had other students asking me to speak to tutors, telling me about the problems they were having, a good thing then that the university had an internal phone system...

Anthony Fox

Critical Thinking

This is one of the most important skills that students need to master at university. Many students fail because they are unaware of the importance placed on critical thinking by universities. The skills you need to master are not taught either through college, at undergraduate study or even at any post graduate level; yet, it is an academic prerequisite in many cases to passing assignments and more importantly exams and ultimately achieving success in your chosen degree.

Anyway, do not fall into the same trap that many other students do at university, and get caught, hook, line and sinker into believing you know what critical thinking is, only to find out that you don't know. It reminds me of the quote by Albert Einstein, "A *little knowledge is a dangerous thing. So is a lot.*"

While attending academic meetings as part of my role as a student representative I found out that students were achieving poor marks or failing assignments and exams because many students failed to understand what critical evaluation meant. Course tutors constantly discussed the students' lack of understanding critical evaluation at these academic meetings which I attended. You need to understand what critical thinking is and know how you need to approach the subject. Examples will be provided so that you can clearly understand critical thinking and evaluation.

I have described critical thinking in the terms expected from you at university level, but this chapter is only a brief instruction on the subject. There are many books that are worth reading if you want to master critical thinking to a professional level. Learning to interpret and analyse other people's work will form a major part of your marks when you have to present an argument for an exam or assignment. Hopefully this brief explanation and example of how to approach critical analysis will help you develop the necessary skills required to reason and argue successfully throughout your academic studies at university.

What is Critical Thinking?

First, let me give you a description from wikipedia.org/Critical_thinking (page accessed, 2009). Critical thinking "*involves determining the meaning and significance of what is observed or expressed, or, concerning a given inference or argument, determining whether there is adequate justification to accept the conclusion as true.*"

What is critical thinking? Many of us can get confused about what it really means. Critical thinking is about evaluating an argument without allowing your beliefs or bias to influence your reasoning whether to support or criticise the argument. Let's face it, we all do it, we get on our soapbox and blast away without first evaluating our argument. It is an easy trap to fall into, where we hold one particular belief and then support another similar belief without first evaluating the supporting evidence. Critical thinking or evaluation is the ability to fairly analyse and evaluate the work of others. The reasoning and argument presented by the author must be well structured with supporting argument and evidence. The ability to use the arguments of other people's work, whether it is a written work, computer code, original music, a work of art, any other original creative idea or even a thought, and to present their argument or reasons for supporting a view, is the art of critical thinking. But the author may have relied on false evidence or assumptions in forming the argument, so it is up to you to ascertain in your analysis why this is true or not by presenting contrary evidence and reasoning in your critical analysis. Often an author will present a position, based on a series of propositions, which support the reasoning behind the argument which the intended audience follows in a logical order, ending with a conclusion.

Students rarely have the time to fully research a particular concept or idea and often have to rely on the work of others to support their view. Critical thinking is essentially the ability to 'read between the lines' and determine what the reasoning is behind the author's argument in support of this argument or to criticise its proposition. A proposition is a statement(s) describing the argument or reasons that support the premise the author is expressing which may be true or false.

Many students seem to think that critical analysis just involves presenting a series of facts in support of an argument without necessarily presenting the reasoning behind the argument. Making arguments based on assertions or assumptions is a common mistake made by many students who failed to handle critical analysis. Assertions are statements that don't have supporting evidence or reason - just as assumptions are ideas or thoughts which we make without a basis of truth that are conjecture.

How to Approach Critical Thinking and Analysis
By using the following method you can easily construct an evaluation and present reasoning for supporting or criticising the argument in a structured manner following a conclusion. This method is a way of

approaching critical analysis under exam conditions, but you may have a different method or adapt this example to suit your style of working. Whatever style you decide to use, this method will at least show you how to quickly understand how to approach critical thinking and analysis in a structured manner. The following steps will help you critically analyse under time constraints.

Below is an example of how I would approach a critical analysis task, which often requires time management skills while under the pressure of exam conditions.

Example:

Step 1:

First choose an argument and read it through several times. Make notes of the main reasoning and the evidence.

Step2:

Make notes about the main argument that are as brief as possible. It's all right to have an opposing view as long as you can back it up with supporting evidence.

Step3:

Evaluate the conclusion.

Step4:

Make a brief note of the conclusion.

Step5:

Formulate your critical analysis by asking yourself why you support or criticise the argument and then support your view with your reasoning, based on supporting evidence and argument.

Once you have taken these steps you will have time to structure your critical evaluation into a logical order and present your view with confidence. When you present your conclusion you will be able to express your view in terms of supporting or criticising the author's argument.

This approach is very useful when dealing with time constraints in exams and thus allows you to flush out the main points and make sense of the arguments presented. The point of using this structure is that it allows you to interpret the argument and present the reasoning in a logical order.

Conclusion

Try to remember it is your bias that leads you astray and your assumptions that cloud your memory. Otherwise, it is a bit like learning a new phone number; it's not long before you've forgotten the old one. Do not take anything I say as gospel, try it, if it works, great, but remember we don't all walk the same path, each of our journeys are different.

In my view, critical evaluation can be used in any situation where you need to present an argument, not just in the classroom. Being able to argue your case is something we do not always have to employ a lawyer for, but there are occasions when we should. Bear in mind, we do not all wear the same shoes. Skills take time, but we can all learn to have a more balanced view. Writing a letter of complaint, negotiating, and verbally presenting our argument are skills we can use every day. So before you get on that soapbox think about what you want to say. We all make mistakes but remember those wise words of Theodore Roosevelt who said, *"The man who makes no mistakes does not usually make anything."* The following story will explain.

There's a Bit More Meat on the Bone

So now you know what it's all about? Well it's never that simple, there's always a bit more meat on the bone and we all have that bias that I talked about earlier to deal with. So let me tell you what happened to me, this may help explain.

It was early on in my education that I got a severe shock to my senses. I was the quiet type ready to listen to just about anyone; that was the problem, yet I didn't know it. College was a new haven where you got to meet new friends; I enjoyed the lifestyle – beer, girls, and the night life, but I hated the work. Well who doesn't, right, it's a shock to the system and you soon have to knuckle down or you flunk out.

Everything was faster there, that's for sure, in and out of different classrooms. Talking about fast, everyone has met them, the guys and girls who talk faster than everyone else and seem smarter than just about everyone else. Smart arses or geeks, they're everywhere, from the factory floor to the apartment store and they have more mouth than a Bigfoot. In some ways, you can't help but listen, everyone crowds round them and you might hope that something will rub off on you. Anyway that's the theory.

Well I knew one all right, you can call him Tim, that's not his real name but it does rhyme with dim and don't take me wrong, he was bright, just not all of the time. Tim was a typical geek with glasses that matched his image of talking the talk and walking the walk. Maybe I'm being a bit hard on the lad, looking back I think he would agree he was a geek who couldn't shut up, but he was still a likeable lad who was sometimes funny. Making friends with Tim was more by accident you could say than by design. I ended up working with Tim and another lad on one of those group projects that are assigned to you by a tutor at college.

You know, sometimes you should listen to that gut feeling (intuition) that is telling you something is not quite right, instead of going headlong with the talking and walking and then not believing you're wrong until you fail.

We failed miserably. I remembered questioning Tim before we started and finished about whether we were on the right track, but there's the bias, I believed what Tim said. I mean he sounded so right and he was definitely smart, well, at least that's what I thought at the time. That's the rub though; just because someone's smart doesn't mean that they're always right and this is what I mean by the bias. I let it get in the way of my reasoning and let it railroad me in to believing that Tim was right. When we got to see the tutor we didn't get the poor mark that I'd expected from him, we got absolute zero. We failed to hit the ball park, we didn't even warrant any score, as a team we scored zilch.

This made sure that now, I always *read between the lines* and determine what the reasoning is behind the author's argument in support of this argument or to criticise its suggestion. Otherwise, remember, we grow up with what I call *excess baggage* that we can get from our parents, our schools and also from our friends and foes, and it takes hard work to negate it from our reasoning to form an honest opinion without bigotry or bias.

Remember, when you're asked to critically analyse or to apply critical thinking in any situation, always read twice through what you are being asked to evaluate. Don't get ahead of yourself, always stop and think first. When you have done this task make notes of the argument presented and of its reasoning and support your evaluation or criticism with relevant evidence in your evaluation. It's all right sometimes to have an opposing view as long as you can back your argument with reasoning and relevant evidence.

So don't get caught in that trap of allowing your assertions or bias to railroad your logic. I've had to stop myself many a time from getting on that old soapbox, so think before you leap. We all make assumptions but not always the right one.

Time Management

Time management is another skill that you need to acquire if you are to reach your goals without experiencing the stress that obtaining a higher education places on you. Many students fail to reach their goals simply because they don't see the importance of planning their study time effectively. As a student representative there were many occasions when students would be seeking my support, requesting tutors to extend assignment deadlines, often with spurious excuses.

Tutors did sometimes extend deadlines if students had genuine problems caused by the university computer systems or conflicting assignment deadlines. But most of the time students just had poor time management which led to tasks not being finished on time and ultimately failure. In some circumstances this led to students having to retake whole semesters.

Time management is one of the key skills that successful people use both at their work and in their personal life. I have provided an example study plan of how to manage your time more effectively. This example you can use and adapt to suit. Planning is an important part of any goal that you set yourself. When you have limited time at university and wish to avoid failure, remember, do not rush headlong into your university education without planning ahead. Even if you don't always strictly follow the plan, the fact you have one will help you gain that edge at university.

Key Skills

Time management is a key skill which you will most certainly need in the work place. Getting used to planning your schedule will lessen the stress that a busy working environment can place on you.

Management of your time will improve your overall performance. Coping with projects on a limited time frame is a pressure, but one that can be managed successfully when pre-planned.

A more managed and organised approach to your studies will improve your performance and lessen the stress of a hectic workload. There's nothing worse than being disorganised and not knowing your progress. This can easily lead to failure.

Note: I found organising my workload was a lot less stressful than would have been the case if I hadn't taken the time to plan my study time.

Create a Study Plan

Creating a study plan is essential so that you can allocate your time more effectively between assignments and the all-important revision for exams. Make your plan in sensible time frames giving adequate space for overruns which are likely to occur.

The following example shows a two month window, usually applicable in the May - June period when exams and assignments are due in around the same time. I created a time management plan using two A4 sheets of white paper sellotaped together. I created the plan below using tables on my laptop but if you prefer you can just use a ruler and sketch it out, then

How to Pass a Degree with Confidence

stick it on the wall somewhere which will remind you every day of what you must to do.

Note: I stuck my study plan right above the computer so it would remind me each day what the schedule was like. It helped me maintain my focus on my studies.

	May				June			
	Week 1	Week 2	Week 3	Week 4	Week 1	Week 2	Week 3	Week 4
Module 1 Assignment							Due June 22	
Module 2 Assignment					Due June 4			
Module 3 Assignment							Due June 16	
Module 4 Assignment				Due May 29				
Module 5 Assignment			Due May 22			Exam June 10		
Revise Module A					Exam June 4			
Revise Module B							Exam June 16	
Revise Module C						Exam June 10		
Revise Module D								

Figure 2: Example Study Plan

Whatever you do at least with this study plan you will have a working idea of when assignments and exams are due. The idea is that you can work out how much time you can allocate for revision for exams and what time you have for assignments. This is not a rigid plan but a working one where you can allow for overruns. With this plan you will have a better chance of coping with the hectic time frame of exams and assignments which often occur at the same time. I used time management plans throughout my years at university as an essential tool in handling a hectic schedule.

Note: Successful projects depend on pre-planning. Always remember that any planning will have overruns and this should be allowed for in your schedule.

Sat There Like a Cheshire Cat

Time management is not just about creating fancy time study plans, which is all well and good if the back end is not protected. Let me tell you a story of what not to do. It happened to me and I hope you don't fall prey to the same disaster. It took place early on in my educational rise to the top. I was deep in the throes of doing an HND (Higher National Diploma) which is one rung below a BSc degree. I was studying computing, or should I say learning how to program computers and about all kinds of weird and wonderful computer languages. I had learnt early on from a young and clever tutor the importance of study plans and how to manage time more effectively.

This tutor spoke about how creating study plans had saved his arse more times than he could remember when he was at university studying for his degrees. I could relate to this wise advice and see the potential of being organised in what you are doing, after all that's how businesses work, and the people employed in those companies follow these plans every day in the work environment. It made sense to me because I had been used to work schedules, coming from a business background, so study plans were just another way of planning that precious study time. But the young and clever tutor forgot to mention one important aspect, which is often the case when all you can see is the forest full of trees. We all do it, for some reason we forget the obvious, and plough head long into disaster. Because it's Sod's Law, Murphy's Law, or the Mother-in-Law that what will go wrong will. It happens all the time, we don't plan for the worst scenario but it happens more times than I care to remember. Have you figured it out yet? Well, you soon will.

It was one of those days when I was doing well and the code I had written and tested was achieving the objectives of the assignment. I was very pleased with myself; sat there like a Cheshire cat with a smile so broad you'd have thought I'd just invented the wheel. Wheel or no wheel, disaster struck with no warning almost as if I'd tempted the Gods. The Gods had taken the smile off of my face faster than I can eat a McDonald's burger, and that's pretty quick! It was all gone, disappeared like a ship in the Bermuda Triangle. I just couldn't believe my eyes, all the Turbo Pascal code I had written had vanished and all I'd done was inadvertently touch a key on the keyboard somewhere I shouldn't have. To be honest I wasn't sure what had happened; all I knew was that all my hard work had disappeared into the ether. The thing was Turbo Pascal had its own operating system so it worked separate to the Windows 95 operating system which was the current model at the time. The Turbo Pascal operating system was held on a 3.5 floppy disc and worked as a layer on top of the Windows 95 operating system. It was several hundred lines of code that went down the Swannee and I was right up the creek without a paddle. Yes! You guessed it. I hadn't bothered to save my code to a different location along the way. So I had to spend the rest of the day re-writing the code from memory which wasn't easy, to say the least. It was a right pain in the butt, but from then on I made sure I kept saving my code. It was a big lesson to learn just one day before the assignment was due in.

Talk about learning lessons, it took another disaster several years later and a magnitude higher for me to really learn my lesson. And, strangely enough it was not long after I had finished my master's degree in Software Engineering in Artificial Intelligence while I was writing this book that another disaster happened just as

I was several thousand words into writing this book. And it wasn't that I hadn't been saving my work. No. It was the dreaded sound of, *'cluck...cluck,'* and the hard drive failing on my laptop, which was only a few months old. So now I save my work religiously and I have a three prong defence against disaster which is I save my work all the time not just to the hard drive, but to a separate floppy drive and I send an email of my work to myself every day. In other words, be prepared for the worst because it's likely to happen when least expected and more than likely at the wrong time. There is no point in having a time management plan in place and working if a disaster could just turn everything upside down in a matter of seconds.

Technology is not infallible and will often let you down when you're least prepared. Hopefully this won't happen to you, or it shouldn't if you've taken precautions. The number of businesses I found who hadn't bothered to back up their data to different sources was relatively high. This was a common theme which always surprised me, considering how important business or personal data is when disaster strikes.

Exam Preparation

You can never spend enough time preparing for those crucial exams, but because of the hectic student life at university this is not always possible. So the next best approach is to make a study plan, which will help you focus the time you have in a more productive way.

Keeping to a study plan will help you to maintain your focus while multi-tasking assignment commitments, exam preparation, and a busy social life. Organising the time you have available will help build the confidence you need on your actual exam day.

Note: Making a study plan helped me allocate the time I had available between exam preparation and on-going course assignments. By determining these into a structure I was able to deal with a demanding schedule without losing focus, and therefore I was a lot more confident when it came to taking my exams.

Create an Exam Revision Study Plan

The following exam revision study plan is simple to construct, whether created using tables or by paper and pencil. Whatever you do, be realistic about how much time you allow for exam revision; don't forget that by then you will most likely have other assignments to work on.

You need to decide how much time you allocate to any particular module or subject. The main object is that you are planning your day to allow enough time for revision and assignments. A structure like a study plan gives you the freedom to design an effective revision timetable so that you are well prepared for exams.

Example: Exam Revision Study Plan

The following example used below is how I allocated time slots to suit my needs. Whatever you decide to use, this tool allows you to focus on multi-tasking in the difficult and hectic environment of universities.

Study Plan	Week 2	Week 3	Week4	Week1	Week 2	Week3	Week 4
Module A	1 hr a day	1 hr a day	1 hr a day	2 hrs a day	3 hrs a day	June 16th Exam	
Module B	1 hr a day	1 hr a day	1 hr a day	2 hrs a day	3 hrs a day	June 17th Exam	
Module C			1 hr a day	2 hrs a day	2 hrs a day	3hrs a day	June 22nd Exam
Module D	2 hrs a day	2 hrs a day	3 hrs a day	June 4th Exam			

Figure 3: Exam Revision Study Plan

Note: I had to make sure I could revise each day while at the same time working on assignments in progress. This approach certainly helped me become mentally prepared and confident when going into exams.

How to Revise

We do not all wear the same shoes so be sure to adapt your revision technique so it best suits your needs. I find the best way to revise is in small allotted time slots based on the study plan that I have created for myself. I use small time slots because this way you are more likely to absorb information. I take each module or subject which I have to revise for and calculate a realistic overall time frame. Then I divide this overall time into slots over the weeks or days that I have to prepare for the exam. Normally you have to revise exams at the same time, juggling assignments and such so it's important you start your preparation early enough. One to two months before exams are due might be my recommendation.

The day before an exam you must relax and revise what you can. Hopefully if you have kept to the plan you will go into the exam feeling confident.

Note: I found it useful to plan these time slots for revision, even though I had plenty of other assignments on the go at the same time to contend with. The process of creating a plan I found helped lessen the stress of commitments and maintain focus.

We Have All the Time in the World

All the time in the world, that's what I thought, as I sat there revising for the following day's exam. I should say this story is a reminder to me and maybe to others not to get too cocky. I made this mistake in my first year in the HND (Higher National Diploma) computing course I was studying at Plymouth University. Computers had always been in my blood from the very first day when many years before I'd started to learn computer programming.

Nowadays, I find technology unreliable because of the frustrations and mishaps I have suffered along the way. I think most people rely on technology too much, thinking it's infallible, but it's not. Not only that, my computer was more likely to break down than a patient on anti-depressants and needing daily psychiatric assistance. Talk about manic; I don't know who's more insane, my computer box, or me for putting up with the constant attention.

It was tough that year, re-adjusting to the rigour of knuckling down to some serious exertion, when all I really wanted to do was to watch a flick or two and swallow a few beers. Life on the inside and life on the outside was how I viewed my predicament. On the outside you have all the distractions you could think of, such as beer, girls and just about anything else you could get your hands on. The inside of university life was very different; you had timetables, lectures and tutorials and a whole lot more of what appeared like organised chaos. At times, it felt like you were chasing yourself, and your shadow couldn't quite keep up. One minute you're dashing from lecture room to another the other side of the university with only minutes to spare. You were like ants gone completely mad in and out in a desperate dash in no particular order. But I was confident and relaxed and had revised for the exam the following day. You have to be confident; that's the first rule of success. The subject matter was new to me, but that's the challenge. I already knew the format of the exam; everyone knew it was going to be a multiple choice exam.

Personally, I had never liked multiple choice exams and because this was the first year of the HND programme and also a mid-term exam I thought it would be a piece of cake. After all, I had spent the time revising the subject for several weeks, but with the added pressure of other assignments to submit and other exams to revise for maybe I didn't give it the attention it deserved, but I still felt confident. But they threw in a spanner into the works, which is what always seems to happen when you are not fully prepared. Something I hadn't figured on. The scenario never crossed my mind. The possible answers were so close together it was difficult to make a positive decision for each question, and there's the rub. Time was running out and I hadn't answered all the questions. It almost got to the point of going *eeny meeny miny mo*, and hoping for the best. I'm glad I didn't gamble, even though I remember not answering all the questions. The questions I did answer I got enough right to just about pass, and at the same time learnt a valuable lesson. Don't take anything for granted and revise until your eyes are popping out of your head, not literally of course. I remember what my dad would say to me; *'Don't take anything for granted son.'* I have to say though, how often do you listen to your dad? I mean I have trouble listening to myself, let alone my parents.

How to Research

There is the right place and time for essential research reading for your dissertation or project. I would always make notes as I read through the information. I would also prefer to have no outside distractions, especially when reading, so that the mind can assimilate information more easily. I believe you can take in the information easier without extra noise blocking your mind. But whatever suits you best, as long as your mind can absorb the information.

You have to decide in any research project which side of the fence you are on. Most of the information you are gathering will fall on one side or the other, so it is up to you to decide where your research should take you. As long as you keep to the objectives and clearly present the relevant evidence to support your research and given view then there should be no problem.

It's all right to have an opposing view as long as you have the relevant research to support this proposition, and can clearly demonstrate this in your project or dissertation.

Organisation plays a key role in effective research; maintaining a file and folder structure, and also a hardbound notebook and a diary which all combine to provide you with effective research.

What to Do

What type of material should you read as part of your research? I would often read the synopsis to get a quick idea if the research paper was worth reading. You can't read everything you find in the process of your research. I had a list of objectives to fulfil in my research project, so this was always there to guide this area of the project. I followed the same method I had used many times before for assignments, as this was just another scale higher in terms of the amount of research required. I bought a hard binding notebook, something which would take some amount of bashing for the weeks ahead in and out of libraries and the general wear and tear of constant handling. I found that I needed two hard binding notebooks for my dissertation research.

Sometimes the most difficult part was leaving the library while there was so much to read that was worth reading. But organisation was an essential key, being able to locate and cite authors with ease because all the information was correctly contained in a notebook which proved an important tool. These steps save a lot of time when you are writing up your project or dissertation.

Note: Each time you make an entry of important information that you might later use in your project or dissertation into the notebook fully cite where you found the information and then record the date that you found the information. That is why my notebook also became a diary recording my research effort. The idea is you then have all the correct information all in one place ready to use and then you'll be able to correctly cite your dissertation or project document at a later date, should you need to.

Choose Your Method

Any research method is valid as long as it fulfils the criteria you have set for the project. A list of specific objectives keeps you on the right track. Following the objectives helps you to read only what is valid when proving or disproving your idea or view within the project or dissertation.

It's easy to miss your objectives when your research takes an interesting turn and one that maybe by reading the evidence would suggest a different approach. But it may be too late during the project's or dissertation's life cycle to change paths. So remember to stick to your objectives and save the other story you may have found for another day.

Remember effective organisation by using folders allows us to quickly retrieve what we need with hardly any effort.

Note: A clear list of objectives previously agreed with your tutor is a good starting point; otherwise the temptation of reading other interesting topics could lead you off of the beaten track. I often found this the case, as the following story explains.

Anthony Fox

We Don't All Wear the Same Shoes

We don't all wear the same shoes, otherwise mine are size eights and that would be boring. Anyway, I've got a story to tell so pull up a chair you coffee junkies, milkshake hussies and tele-tubbies. It began when I was deep in the labyrinth of rooms in the University of Sunderland's library researching the dissertation for my masters. It was like a subterranean cave in some ways, but the walls were lined with books to the ceiling with racks upon racks of more books that formed the labyrinth of passageways.

I was submerged in my quest to find information to support my thesis. I would often spend my day making notes and reading as much as I could in the little time that I had. But I enjoyed what I was doing; it became my second home where I was surrounded with a wealth of knowledge at my fingertips. I would often stray off the track leading down a path which I didn't need to go, but I couldn't help myself, sometimes the stories I read were just too interesting to discard. I felt like an investigative reporter finding a story for the first time and all I could do was keep chasing the story. There seemed to be a common theme in what I was reading, but it wasn't directly related to the research I was undertaking and yet it plays a role in all our lives whether we like it or not.

As the days and weeks passed time and time again the same theme would emerge as I made my way through the mountain of books and research papers. I wasn't looking for it, but it was there starring me in the face, a colossus that I couldn't avoid. I was consumed as a junkie is on heroin, an insatiable appetite to know more, I was hooked and there was no going back. I had to understand the reasons why, but I guess I already knew and I just couldn't believe it. Plus as I was researching my dissertation, this story I had stumbled on wasn't directly related, but in a way it affected us all, we just don't know or understand the reasons why. Somehow, I knew I would include the story in my dissertation, I just didn't know to what level.

Understanding what the theme now was I could pinpoint within a few words what it was that caused so much tragedy and heartache in the world. The American soldiers who lost their lives operating the Patriot system defending Israel from SAM missiles being launched by Iraq forces is one example. The American astronauts who lost their lives in that costly NASA space mission that went so wrong are another. Also how the Ariane 5 rocket launch in 1996 turned into a disaster costing 7 billion dollars. The innovative Iridium satellite phone company that went bust costing billions of dollars for the original investors is another. Of course there are still many, many more costly examples and sometimes tragic loss of life which maybe could have been avoided if we'd understood that it's human nature and the weak points of projects that can cause the disasters.

All these disasters and more had one common denominator, and that was having a weak point and human nature failing to see this. We overlook the obvious sometimes and it's the weak points that then let us down. We don't all wear the same shoes and we can't always see the forest for the trees.

Writing Your Dissertation Project

One of the most demanding tasks you will have to accomplish is writing that winning dissertation which forms such a critical part of your final marks towards getting that master's degree. Even if you are not attempting a master's degree the same steps that are necessary apply equally to preparing your final project for a bachelor's degree. So I will prepare you for the task in hand; because of the academic weighting placed on a dissertation or final project, it's critical for you to achieve your goal of passing and not failing this final task.

Having to write a 20,000 word dissertation will, for too many, seem a daunting task, especially for those who have never compiled a 20,000 word document before. But have no fear; the following information in the sub-headings below will make the task a lot less daunting.

In any project there is always a planning stage. You should create a time management plan using a Gant chart to structure and organise what time you have. In any plan you can overrun the allotted time you have allocated, but it's still a useful guide, to be able to see your progress at any given time, and how you may have to speed up if you want to stick to your original plan.

This plan should be divided into appropriate time slots, such as weeks. The chart should also be colour coded, so that each stage of the time planning stands out over the coming weeks of the time frame. Whatever you do, make sure you stick to your plan, and that it's as realistic as possible.

Note: I found it useful to create a Gant chart with Microsoft excel rather than use some other bespoke software. I didn't want to spend hours preparing a chart with fancy software when a simple solution was just as good for my needs. I decided to divide my chart into weeks since I only had three months to work on my dissertation. I considered that I would need at least three weeks to write up my dissertation, allowing for corrections and final proof reading. I also considered that the dissertation project would take at least eight weeks of research and development. This left one week of slack which I could use for overrun or if I needed more time for the final write up.

I also found using a Gant chart proved a useful tool to guide my progress as the weeks appeared to pass quicker than they seemed, so it was always there to keep my eye on the objectives. Another tip - I stuck the Gant chart right where I could see it every day, right in the middle on the top of my computer.

Buy yourself a hard bound A4 size note book to use as a personal diary and as somewhere you can collate information in one organised space. You will find this a useful tool when you are researching information in libraries as it's easier to make and later find your notes. On a daily basis it helps to keep a diary of your progress.

Note: I didn't go anywhere without my red hardbound diary while I was researching and reading journals and books in libraries. It also became a place where I could make a note of any reference that I might want to use at a later date. Accessing online data also meant I kept an accurate record of the date when I accessed the information. In the end I had to buy another hard bound A4 note book as the first one I had completely filled up.

Preparation

Always back your work up in several different places. Floppy disc, email or separate hard disc, anything away from your usual working equipment. What will go wrong usually does when you're least prepared. So always be prepared for the worst that can happen so when it does you have the backup there to save the day. You can avoid the scenario of losing your work the day before submission this way.

Note: I would send emails to myself containing the main dissertation or project document, this way I had an incremental account to refer to if needed at a future date. The most important aspect of sending emails to yourself is not relying on hardware that could let you down right when you need it. I just couldn't take the chance of hardware failure, so it became a habit to send daily emails, that way I was always protecting my back end, also meaning I could get a good night's sleep.

Good preparation is important right from the outset, so you should create a folder structure for your project or dissertation that allows you to organise and find documents when needed. The following example is from my dissertation project.

Figure 4: Dissertation Folder Structure

Note: I started my folder structure right at the beginning of the project and built it up from there, as and when needed. Creating a folder structure made me feel organised and confident about the way ahead. The project was going forward and not the other way. By doing this you will find it easy to find documents when you need them, rather than wasting precious time finding them.

Proposal

The dissertation project proposal can either be one of the hardest or one of the simplest tasks to undertake. The proposal will have to be approved by a senior lecturer or a department head of your faculty. Normally some project and dissertation proposals are automatically listed for consideration by department heads or senior lecturers for you to consider and undertake. It is always important to embark on a project that best suits you and is something that you will find interesting, otherwise you will most likely struggle and it will show in what you submit.

Note: If you are stuck as to what to propose as a suitable dissertation project, then the best way would be to ask a suitable department head or senior lecturer for a likely project you could choose. They usually have many useful ideas which you might want to consider. I personally used this approach and adapted the idea suggested to suit the ideas and thinking more towards what I was interested in. Of course any project proposal would still have to be approved by the appropriate department head or senior lecturer for a final dissertation project.

Terms of Reference

The term of reference document is a document that outlines the boundaries and the objectives of the dissertation project. It is a document which usually requires submission to the assigned project sponsor who will then have to sign the document before the dissertation project can begin. Each university will have their own set procedure but you should be fully informed of what you need to do. Essentially this document, whatever it is called, will outline the boundaries and the main objectives of the dissertation project under the guidelines set out by the university.

Note: I found this document took time to construct before I had a clear and succinct outline of the project. I remember having to revise this document a couple of times before it was approved by the project sponsor. You normally need references in your document to make your argument and case for the project dissertation and also a list of objectives that should stay well inside the boundaries of the project. Don't make the mistake of taking on more than you can chew in the time that you have.

List the Objectives

The list of objectives is an important aspect of the project or dissertation. It is this that will determine the boundaries of the dissertation. Do not list objectives that are unachievable within the time frame of the project or your capabilities. Tutors who mark your dissertation or project will judge your performance partially based on these objectives.

Eventually tutors will mark your project according to the list of objectives you originally submitted. Check if you've achieved all or most of your project objectives and be careful you're not stretching yourself. Speak to your tutor or project supervisor and ask their advice before you submit a list of objectives you can't fulfil.

Note: I found that a maximum of ten objectives were achievable in the time frame allotted for the dissertation, and it's difficult enough to successfully achieve this many. So be careful!

How to Write

I found one of the best ways to approach writing a dissertation project was to decide the initial structure and use this as the starting point. As you decide what the main chapters are you can then decide what the sub-headings are and so on. Using this technique is the simplest and best way of approaching writing a 20,000 word dissertation or project. For any project you will need a starting point and as it progresses you should add to the structure, which will then have a balance that you can adjust, as you feel necessary.

Note: If you keep an ordered folder structure like I previously mentioned you will be able to retrieve documents when necessary without having to waste time looking for them. An organised approach right at the beginning of the dissertation project will mean a well-structured dissertation throughout the time frame of the project. An example of this approach is how I kept a note of every reference with full citation in a red hard bound diary as I read each book, journal or online resource with a note of the idea, concept or findings of the original author and whether or not I used that reference in my dissertation. This way I always knew where to find the references for future use. Another tip is that I would write the references into a reference document in my dissertation as I went along, so that the tedious task was done way before the rush at the end. This process saves loads of time later, like when you have to compile references for the dissertation. The process is laborious so it's easier to do it as you go along.

Review your Dissertation or Project

When you've finished your writing, have one or two of your colleagues review and read your dissertation. It helps to have a different set of eyes see your work and so does useful criticism. Believe me, it's a useful advantage to have some feedback before you actually submit your work.

Print out your dissertation at least once so that you can proof read your document, looking for obvious grammatical mistakes and corrections, after which comes the final print.

Note: I sent my dissertation to two friends on the course and reviewed their work also. This process was very useful because having two different opinions evened out the bias to a certain degree. My friends were glad I did them a favour and I was glad they did me a favour. All in all it was a useful process.

How to Approach Your Viva
Remember there are two parties involved in the viva, which is you and the independent tutors marking you; it's an easy trap to present your viva without considering that the tutors will not have spent the time that you have on your project or dissertation. Your presentation notes should be clearly visible by your preamble to give any spectator the ability to get up to speed with what your project is about. Most vivas will involve the use of a PowerPoint presentation, which should also allow the spectator the ability to clearly understand what your dissertation is all about. It's also important that your PowerPoint presentation is not too long and not too short, allowing enough time for each slide to form an impression on the spectator.

Another important point is to try not to get nervous; remember your spectators want to be relaxed and enjoy the presentation as well, and the more nervous you are the more they will feel uncomfortable. Take a deep breath before you start and try not to rush yourself. Take your time. You will have practised your presentation and allowed enough time to finish within the allotted time frame, usually about half an hour. You can always crack a joke if it relates to your project, and is recommended if it helps to relax the atmosphere. Smile and speak calmly using your presentation notes to guide you through the slides. Whatever you do, take your time and make the information you are trying to convey as interesting as possible for your audience.

Note: When I practised my viva presentation I realised that I had too many PowerPoint slides, so I had to discard these and re-do it before my time limit ran out. That is the point of practising your presentation. I also got a friend to judge my performance which helped me to fine tune it. This process helped me get rid of some of my nerves.

A Girl Came Knocking on My Window
 This reminds of the time I was busy polishing off the final stages to my dissertation when a certain young lady came knocking at my window. My post graduate on campus digs was a room which had just about enough space to have a couple friends round to swing a few beers. At the time my girlfriend would stay over on the weekends in my pad, which was pretty nice even in the single bed we shared, although I don't think she was best pleased when a young blonde came knocking at my window. My girlfriend was a brunette and I guess she saw the blonde as competition. Wouldn't you feel the same? She was a German girl and she had that kind of authority in the way she spoke English that reminds you that she was German all right, something you can't forget. In some ways her voice was sexy in a kind of

masochistic way, not that I like to be whipped into submission. She was a typical German, if there is such a thing. She was a blue eyed blonde, with that jaunty look that said everything about her. I can't remember exactly the title of the masters' she was studying, only from being bored out of my mind from reading the importance of '*working in groups*,' which seemed to be repeated hundreds of times. I believe her masters' title was in Humanities.

Anyway, she looked pretty distressed at the window so I told her to come round to the front of the apartment block and I would buzz her in; I don't think my girlfriend was best pleased. I guess she was thinking: *How often does this happen?* The German girl's name I've forgotten but let's call her Karen. Before I continue with the story, I have to ask one question. Why is it that blondes always turn up when the girlfriend is in residence, never on those other lonely nights? I guess it's Sod's Law, Murphy's Law, or the blonde law that says turn up when the girlfriend's there, otherwise forget he's there. Which I think pretty much sums it up.

Anyway, Karen was fretting about her dissertation and she wanted me to take a look to try and help her through the quagmire she had dug for herself. I guess she thought being mature I could help, but I really couldn't afford to waste the time helping her. I told her I would take a look at her dissertation to see what I thought. My girlfriend who was a qualified lawyer thought the same as me. Karen's dissertation didn't come up to scratch in our opinion. You could see where one author descended into another, the mash of Karen's English grammar was obvious. She had plagiarised a lot from what we could see, and although she could speak good English, her written English didn't match up, especially at masters' level. We just couldn't believe what we were looking at; in our opinion it was a miss-mash of authors and it was miles too long, way beyond the 20,000 words criteria. And the constant ramble of the same old theme was a persistent reminder. The dissertation was in a bad state, we couldn't see any way she would even pass and that was being honest. Karen was lucky my girlfriend was there and was willing to spend a few hours whipping the dissertation into some kind of shape.

After I had spent an hour on it and my girlfriend several more, we handed the dissertation back to Karen to complete but we still had the same opinion about whether Karen would pass or not. Besides being pessimistic about Karen's chances my girlfriend wasn't willing to spend any more time doing her work. I don't blame her for that; I felt the same. We did our best for a friend and it was now up to Karen to do the rest.

The irony was that I heard some time later that Karen scored a first in her masters. What she did I will never know; maybe she got down on her knees and prayed? Anyway, do not leave it to the last moment before you seek advice and help with your dissertation, which is the moral of this story. Karen was lucky my girlfriend and I were willing to give advice and help when it was needed, otherwise the outcome may have been completely different.

Ten Tips for Uni

N0 1: Enjoy it! Above all enjoy your time at university; it's one of the best times of your life. Immerse yourself in as many university activities as possible. If you enjoy your time at university you're halfway there to success.

N0 2: Get to know your student rep. He or she will be the one person who will offer support when you need it most. Your student representative is the link to the university academia and will be able to ask questions on your behalf.

N0 3: Get to know your tutors. Don't be afraid to approach your tutors for advice. Ask questions if you do not understand anything you are asked to do. It's the tutors' job to help their students.

N0 4: Join a university club. There are so many different university clubs you can join, away from the course you are doing. As a way of relaxing and making new friends joining a club will help you deal with stress and build confidence.

N0 5: Do not suffer in silence. Always seek help when you feel you need it. There is a whole host of university facilities available, helping you cope with the stresses and strains of university life. Talk to someone about whatever problem you're facing, even if it's just with a friend. There is always help available no matter what the problem.

N0 6: Do not worry if you fail. If you fail an exam, assignment or even a module, just knuckle down and work harder. Remember it happens sometimes, but we can all rise to the challenge. No journey leads down a straight path, there are always detours. It's how you cope that matters.

N0 7: Apply for free money. Take time to apply for as much free funding that is available to you as you can. The university will be a great source of extra funding and information about where you can apply to external sources, so make the most of the opportunity.

N0 8: Avoid plagiarism. Universities come down harshly on any students found to be plagiarising other people's work. Learn the rules of how to cite your documents to the standards set by your university.

N0 9: Do not cheat. So many students fall into the trap of plagiarism or cheating, and they are only cheating themselves. There are no short cuts in life. Failure with your work is acceptable, it happens sometimes, but hopefully we've done our best; but failure with other people's work is just cheating and lazy.

N0 10: Get plenty of exercise. Make sure you get plenty of rest and exercise. All the hard work will be worth it. Rest and enjoy your free time. Good luck!

How to Cope With Meagre Funds

See your student representative

It's always a good idea to see your student rep as soon as possible to find out what extra funds might be available. Your student rep will be an important link for you throughout your course, so get to know him or her as soon possible. The student rep can at least point you in the right direction to apply for university funds specifically designed for your needs.

University funds

The university should have many separate funds that you can apply for depending on its requirements. So make sure you apply early because these funds usually dwindle pretty quickly. All the effort usually pays off though, so don't get disappointed if your application is turned down, just keep trying. Universities often have funds available mid-term which you can also apply for.

Grants

There are plenty of grants available, but normally you have to be quick to apply. A free bursary is always a good idea, so try and find a university that offers this. It's easy to check online or other media to find the information you require. Some universities inform their students of what grants are available, but I would make sure you do your own ground work and not rely on what they initially tell you; otherwise you could easily lose out on potentially free money.

Charities

Always good sources of potential extra funds are educational charities, but they do have their own criteria as to whether they will make a grant to you. National as well as local charities will have different criteria and rules as to who can apply, but you should easily winkle out the ones that will favour your situation. They may take time to reply sometimes, so don't worry if you haven't heard from them in a while.

Charities have elective boards where members may just meet every couple of months to decide on the merits of a particular candidate for charitable funds, so be patient. The more charities you apply to, the higher the chance that you will receive some extra funds you can spend on yourself rather than just books.

If you do not ask you will not receive

Make sure you ask in several places and don't get disappointed if one avenue becomes a dead end. Losing out on free money you could have had if you'd just asked will bite you in the ass one day when you find your meagre funds have run out. It's all right to ask, so don't worry about asking; the more you find out the more likely the outcome will be that you have money in your pocket.

Getting a part-time job

Getting a part-time job could be one way of making ends meet. But don't let your study time lapse. If you can juggle the two then it could be an enjoyable as well as financially rewarding experience.

What Next

It's a good thing if you've really struggled to get your degree, because it will have prepared you for the real world outside of university life. The next step is to go for that job you were aiming for or maybe to start another degree, hopefully now with confidence.

Remember it won't be easy, whatever you decide to do; nothing worthwhile is easy, it all takes effort and hard work, but now you have the skills and experience to take on the challenge. Whatever you decide, it might be different from your original goal, but that's OK, because life is a journey in which we don't always take the most obvious path to where we're going.

www.ingramcontent.com/pod-product-compliance
Ingram Content Group UK Ltd.
Pitfield, Milton Keynes, MK11 3LW, UK
UKHW041412180426
11947UKWH00007B/88